The Magic Golden Pen and Poems

The Magic Golden Pen and Poems

Written and Illustrated by

By Mark A. Dema, Ph.D

This is a work of fiction. Names, characters, places and incidents either are the product of the author's imagination or are used fictitiously, and any resemblance to any actual persons, living or dead, events, or locales is entirely coincidental.

This book was printed in the United States of America.

To order additional copies of this book, contact:
Xlibris Corporation
1-888-795-4274
www.Xlibris.com
Orders@Xlibris.com
26464

CONTENTS

POEMS

For my Mother and Father

Introduction

Here is a story for children, adults, and senior citizens as well. The quest for immortality is as infinite and endless as the heavens above, and the universe that lies within us, and outside of us. Jonathan is a character who demonstrates that losing a loved one involves losing a part of oneself. We can all identify with that. And like all human beings, Jonathan must learn to come to grips with his own mortality. He develops the virtues of faith, courage, and love. Inevitably, these virtues carry him to the greatest paradise here on earth . . . peace of mind! Like all heroes, his own perseverance will eventually bring him a miracle. It is certain that luck is when opportunity and hard work cross one another's paths. Jonathan gives the reader hope because he has enough faith to follow his dreams, and inevitably those dreams come true.

Chapter I

I could not understand why my mother died. Indeed, it made me sad that people were sort of like flowers. They bloomed into wonderful colors, enriched the world with beauty, then withered, and eventually died. When I went to my mother's wake, it did not look like her in the coffin. She looked more like a waxed doll than a human being. I often wondered what happens to people when they die. It wasn't so much death that frightened and saddened me; it was that unknown realm, beyond death. It was that dimension beyond my imagination that puzzled and perplexed me most. I had the sense my mother's body was only the shell left behind, and my real mother took her smile and essence to another place.

It had been nine months since my mother's passing, and although it still felt like a knife passing through my heart, I tried to think of happy things. My sister, Jasmine, told me she tried to think of all the happy times we shared with mother. Her advice was good, but difficult to put into practice. They say time heals all wounds, but my mother's death was forever.

On a crisp October Sunday afternoon, Jasmine, and my father and I went to an antique shop in London. As we rode along a ribbon of highway, the golden sun burned away a grey fog, and a deep, blue sky appeared. The colorful leaves were dancing and laughing. Orange, red, and yellow foliage rose and fell under the strength of the wind. Squares of white light and black shadows created a checkerboard upon the open road. As we listened to Beethoven's Fifth Symphony, the trees and the wind blended into one. It cheered our hearts.

When we entered the quaint antique shop, Jasmine noticed a golden tipped fountain pen. The pen gleamed from inside a glass showcase. It had a glossy, black body, and its point shined like the golden sun! I peered into the case and said,

"Look, the tip says 14 carat gold upon it." Suddenly, a tall, thin elderly man approached my sister and me. His long hair and beard were as white as snow, and he wore glasses that rested on the tip of his long, pointed nose. Then he said,

"Yes, indeed, that is a beautiful pen, and I might add quite a remarkable one."

"May we see it?" I inquired. He took the pen out of the showcase, and said,

"You pull this side lever to fill it with ink." Then he explained and demonstrated,

"See, you place the point into the bottle of ink, pull out the lever, and the ink is then drawn into the bladder inside the pen."

"Wow, awesome!" my sister and I exclaimed. So we chipped in our money and purchased the pen; it was over fifty years old. As Jasmine grasped the pen, she felt a strange sensation transmitted to her slender fingers.

When we arrived home, we couldn't wait to write with the pen. We sat at Dad's desk and wrote our names.

"How exquisite it writes." We both agreed out loud. And Dad praised its quality,

"Over fifty years old, and that gold pen still can write brilliantly." Then, he added,

"I wouldn't mind using it to illustrate some of my own paintings and cartoons."

My father was a professional cartoonist, as well as a renowned artist, and if he wanted to use the pen, it had to be something special. Jasmine and I decided we would take turns using the pen, and we would do this by using it on alternate days.

Chapter II

The next day, as I ran to class, the fountain pen dropped from my shirt pocket onto the football field. As Jasmine and I sat in math class, I put my little fingers into my shirt pocket, and I was amazed when I could not feel the pen. I poked Jasmine, who sat beside me,

"Jasmine, the pen was right here in my pocket, and now it's gone!"

"Maybe you just misplaced it", she comforted, "don't worry; it will turn up."

Then like a bolt from the sky, I realized I might have dropped the pen onto the football field. Again, I poked my sister in the shoulder, and she said,

"Now what is it? I'm trying to finish these equations before she collects the homework."

I pointed to the long, gothic window, and we looked down upon the field. There upon the soft green the gold tip glittered within the blades of grass. The black cap lay right beside the pen, and the gold tip glinted like a spark of sunshine.

"Look, there it is." I whispered.

"We'll have to get it during lunchtime." She said.

As the morning slipped by, thick, dark clouds gathered into an ominous mass. Suddenly, it was as dark as night. Soon the boom of thunder could be heard from far away. A howling wind blew the dead leaves like sheets of dried paper; they crackled and swirled upon the ground. In a few moments, pouring rain drenched the football field. We stared at one another with a sense of helplessness. All at once, a piercing crack could be heard, and a golden streak of lightning raced to the earth. It struck the pen directly. Both Jasmine and I could feel the buzz right through our own fingertips! The pen lit up like an electric rod. It looked like a sparkler on the fourth of July. Spears of white light shot from the gold tip into the wet, moist air. The luminous point stabbed our eyes. Then, through the dark clouds, a silver streaking light with a red-flamed tail zoomed across the sky; it burst into tiny pieces; it was a shooting star! The storm passed just as quickly as it had come. Jasmine and I were sure the pen was destroyed. When the bell rang, we flew for the football field. The pen was soaked, but still intact. I wiped the droplets of water from the pen with my handkerchief, and screwed the cap on tightly.

Chapter III

That afternoon I had a spelling test. Spelling was my worst subject. Mrs. Parksfield began the test. As she said each word and used it in a sentence, a strange phenomenon occurred. First, the pen gave a slight tingling sensation to my fingers, and then, the correct spelling of every word flowed from the golden tip to the blue lines of the loose-leaf paper. When the tests were corrected, I had scored 100 per cent! I was amazed! I truly believed it was the pen writing the correct answers. It seemed to have its own will, its own power, its own magic!

"Hey, stupid, who are you kidding with that 100% in Spelling?"

It was Butch. He was the, in your face, bully of my entire life. As I stared into his scowling face, bitter memories quickly flowed through my mind. There was the time Butch stuck his foot out in the middle of the class aisle, and I tripped flat on my face. I recalled the humiliation when the entire class laughed at me. For years, Butch had me, and many others, on the run. He would take money, snacks, lunches, and most of all your dreams and dignity.

"What do you mean, Butch?" I said in a husky voice.

"You know what I mean", he said sarcastically, "You're not bright enough to pass any test, let alone spelling." I defended myself, and I said,

"Look, Butch, I studied very hard for that test, and . . ." He cut me off, and said,

"Yeah, Yeah! Look, just make sure you let me know how you did it. I want some 100s too."

Rrrrrring! I was saved by the end of the period bell. I ran quickly to my next class.

That night, before going to bed, I spoke with my sister, Jasmine.

"I'm telling you Jasmine, I never studied those words. It was like the pen knew what to write. The answers seemed to just pour out of the pen." Jasmine raised her eyebrows, and rolled her big eyes towards heaven. And she said,

"Jonathan, you've got some imagination; a pen that writes the correct answers. It's ridiculous!" But I continued to protest,

"But I'm telling you. It was the pen! Why won't you believe me? Look, tomorrow you have a social studies test, right?"

"Yes." She sighed.

"Well", I said, "Try using the pen and see what happens." She looked me squarely in the eye and said,

"I can tell you exactly what is going to happen. I'm going to fail miserably because I didn't study a lick."

And with this final statement, she went to bed. The moon shined like a silver disc, and long lines of silver bars flashed through the chinks of the window blinds. It lit Jasmine's room with pale blue light. As she stared at the pale moonlight, she could not stop thinking about all I had told her. As sleep's gentle fingers closed her weary eyes, she dreamed of the magic golden pen.

The next day, the fog looked like shreds of cotton upon the hills and vales, and a misty rain descended gently. Jasmine took her social studies test during second period. She filled the pen with beautiful royal blue ink. As she did this, once again, the pen sent its strange sensation through her fingers. She received the test, and out of her nervousness, looked it over. The questions looked hard. She thought she would never pass. But when she began to use the pen, the golden tip poured out the blue ink in a dazzling array of correct answers. "Jefferson, Declaration of Independence, 1776, Battle of Saratoga, Minute Men, Nathan Hale, etc." The perfect answers flowed like liquid treasures. It was that defining moment in one's life. A miracle had occurred! It was true! The pen possessed magical powers. Indeed, she realized I was right. The pen spewed correct answers like a volcano. She and I knew that we must keep it a precious secret. No one must ever know!

Chapter IV

The next important test would be in English. Jasmine had difficulty with English, and was desperate to use the pen.

"Jonathan, you know I have more trouble with English than you do." She pleaded, "Please let me use the pen, tomorrow."

"That's just not fair", I argued, "We made a deal to take turns using the pen, and tomorrow is my turn. That's what alternate days mean. In case you didn't know."

"But you're so good at grammar and usage. I'm not. Please, Jonathan." She said.

I just gave her a look of surrender and sighed,

"OK, already, stop begging."

As Jasmine took the test, her joy overwhelmed her. The social studies test was not a coincidence. The pen was for real. It worked its magic in a profound way. It wrote in broad, graceful strokes. The exquisite penmanship made easy work of the most difficult questions. Nouns, verbs, metaphors, conjunctive adverbs, similes were now easy work for Jasmine.

After a few weeks, the entire school buzzed about the tremendous improvement in our grades. I tried to keep it a secret, but teachers talked about it, and friends, as well as those who were envious noticed our test papers when teachers gave them back to us.

One afternoon, as we sat in English class, the principal announced over the P.A.,

"Will Jasmine and Jonathan please come to the office, immediately?"

As we walked into the office, there was Mr. Steele at his huge desk. He sat with a grim look on his pudgy face. His fat cheeks were flushed, and he raised his thick, salt and pepper eyebrows with suspicion. The light above his desk made his bald head shine like a cue ball.

"Well", he said, "I imagine you know why you're here."

We sat there open mouthed, and fearful of what he might actually know. With a hard stare he said,

"It seems both of you have been getting nothing but A's and 100s for the past month. Your teachers feel you have been almost too perfect to believe. Do you have an explanation?" I spoke first,

"Well, sir, we've been studying together a lot." Then Jasmine nudged my leg with her foot under the desk and said, "Tell him how many hours per night we study, Jonathan."

"That won't be necessary." Mr. Steele interrupted, "I just want you to know that if any funny business is going on, you will get caught." Then he added, "If, on the other hand, you are earning these grades on your own merits, I apologize and congratulate both of you."

Jasmine and I nodded, and were happy to leave the office relatively unscathed.

Unscathed that is, until we entered the corridor. There was Butch, with his crew cut, and steady staring eyes.

"I see old, baldy Steele wants to know how you guys do it." He said. He then grabbed me and got right into my face, and threatened me,

"Listen, stupid! I want 100s too, and you better tell me how I can get them." Before I could speak, Jasmine clutched at Butch's arm and said,

"Get your hands off my brother! We don't have to tell you anything. And if you bother us again, Jonathan is going to have to teach you a lesson."

"Wow, I'm shaking with fear." Butch taunted her.

At that moment, two teachers were walking down the hall, and Butch pretended he was on his way to class. As I watched him walk away, I felt awful for not standing up to him. Even worse, my sister had demonstrated more courage than I had.

In the next period, Butch was in Jasmine's Science class. He spied her writing with the odd looking pen. Then, he snatched it from her hand. She reacted vehemently, and said,

"Butch, how dare you! Give it back. That's my special pen!" He teased, and said,

"Hold your horses. I just want to see it." When he noticed Jasmine's anxious face, he said, "Say, what are you so nervous about? Don't tell me this thing has something to do with your grades?" Just as she was about to grab the pen, Mr. Williamture stood towering over the two students.

"What's all the fuss about here?" He asked.

"Nothing, I let Butch use my pen, that's all," she replied.

"Well, let's calm down, and get to work." Mr. Williamture said gently.

In the meantime, Butch could not get the wise smirk off his face. As he began to write with the pen, his arrogance turned to horror. The pen wrote its own special message to him. It wrote:

"You are a little coward,
Who believes he is so cool,
Always picking on gentle people,
But you are nothing but a fool.

When Jonathan sees his true strength,
His courage and fidelity,
Then you will humble yourself,
Singing a kinder melody!"

Butch tapped my sister's shoulder, and showed her his notebook.

"Jasmine, you gotta be kidding", he exclaimed, "this stupid pen actually wrote this! What's going on?"

Jasmine sensed his fear, and took advantage of it. She said confidently,

"I can only tell you my brother and I have been empowered in a most special way. The pen writes only the truth!"

Butch was not to be intimidated and he replied,

"Yeah right . . . . well suppose I take the dumb pen, and crush it under my heel. No more pen, and no more power for you and your stupid brother!"

Quite suddenly, the pen threw out an electric charge. It was like the charge that gave Jasmine a tingling sensation when she first touched the pen, only this time far more forceful and painful!

"Ouch!" Butch cried out, and dropped the pen to the floor. Jasmine quickly picked it up. Mr. Williamture, watching the entire scene, became annoyed, and demanded an explanation. But before anyone could answer, the pen began spouting, and squirting ink towards Butch. Jasmine held it in her hand, and tried to stop it, but the pen continued to squirt blue ink all over Butch's face, hair, and clothes. He bolted from the classroom in total humiliation. Mr. Williamture was appalled and demanded to know what happened.

"Jasmine, how did Butch get covered in blue ink?"

"I'm so sorry, Mr. Williamture", she said, "when I picked up the pen, I accidentally pulled this lever, and the ink squirted onto Butch."

"Well, please be more careful next time." He said.

When Jasmine left the class, she was absolutely thrilled. She could not wait to tell me all about it. We wouldn't have to worry about Butch anymore.

Chapter V

On the way home that afternoon, Edgar Simmerson, the genius of Blue Mountain School, sat next to Jasmine on the bus. He was a pudgy boy with carrot colored hair, blue eyes, and a round freckled face. Edgar was not much of an athlete, and not very popular, but he was respected for his wit and intelligence. He had a keen mind, and was great at solving problems. From behind his wire rimmed glasses, he said,

"I have discovered the secret key that can open the door and allow all to see how you and Jonathan earn such high grades." Edgar had gone to private schools in our great England, and had quite a dignified accent.

"Tell me, Edgar, the big know it all of Blue Mountain School". Jasmine answered with icy words. But Edgar responded coolly,

"It was a simple deduction actually; neither one of you has earned high honors before, so I doubt you could change so suddenly, and so drastically. No, only a miracle could help you do that; and, indeed, you received your miracle. That fountain pen of yours."

Edgar had a crush on Jasmine since fifth grade, but she never gave him a speck of attention. Although he was friends with me, she hardly knew Edgar existed. He knew she would pay attention to his astute observation concerning the pen. It meant so much to her.

"Fountain pen?" She acted surprised, and then added, "Edgar you've been Jonathan's friend for a long time. I've always thought you were a little weird, but never crazy."

"Hardly", he said very sure of himself, "you and your brother take turns using the pen, and you only employ it when testing. I've been observing and I believe my hypothesis is correct. That pen is giving you the correct answers for each test. However, my lips are sealed if I can share the good fortune with you and Jonathan."

Jasmine was concerned and Edgar could see it written upon her pretty face. In a strange way he felt sorry for her. He did not want to upset her; he just wanted to use the pen, and show her how smart he was. His heart melted whenever he saw her beautiful green eyes. He so desperately wanted Jasmine to like him.

That night, after dinner, Jasmine told me all about the episode on the bus.

"I know what we can do", I pondered out loud, "We can tell Edgar about how the lightning gave the pen its magic, and now the magic has worn off." Jasmine rolled her eyes, once again, towards the heavens, and said,

"He will never believe it; he's too smart." Eventually, we will have to tell him the truth. And it will have to be soon." Then gathering a momentum of ideas, she said,

"Jonathan, your idea is clever. We will let him see us take our next tests, and we will deliberately fail them.

"Then he's bound to believe the pen has lost its magic." I said, and then added,

"You know, Jasmine, it wouldn't hurt if you were kinder to Edgar. He thinks you're really cute and smart."

By the end of the week, we had convinced Edgar the pen was now ordinary. After two failed tests, and reprimands from our teachers, Edgar now believed our story. We had fooled a genius. How cool was that? Indeed, it was difficult to fail the tests because the pen wanted to write the correct answers. It required deep concentration to put down incorrect answers. In fact even the muscles in our little fingers hurt from maneuvering the pen against its will.

Chapter VI

One day, while doing penmanship, in Mr. Pendleton's class, Edgar asked me if he could use the pen. I did not want Edgar to get suspicious so I said yes. Besides, it was only cursive writing; I did not have to worry about the pen writing correct answers.

As Edgar began the writing exercise, the pen gave him a strange vibration through his thumb and index finger. It frightened him, and as he attempted to copy Mr. Pendleton's perfect chalky letters from the blackboard, the flowing ink wrote this message:

"Go back to the football field,
Where lightning gave me fame,
You will find a piece of a shooting Star
Fallen in my name."
Edgar panicked and nudged me.

"Look", He exclaimed in a loud whisper. "This is what the pen wrote."

I did not question Edgar. I knew how special the pen was. And as the old man had told me when I bought it, "Quite a remarkable pen."

"Let me have the pen so I can see what it will write to me." I said.

As Edgar looked on apprehensively, I held it in my hand, and it began to write:

"A tiny sparkle you will see,
Make a wish to flow inside of me,
As you squeeze the cube of glittering light,
You will liquidize one day and one night.
But before the first rays of the dawn,
You must emerge, or forever be gone."

When the dismissal bell clanged throughout the corridors, Edgar, Jasmine, and I ran to the football field.

"I still think you guys are weird", said Jasmine.

"Look", I sighed, "We didn't ask the pen to write what it did; there has got to be a reason for all this. It made our fingers tingle when holding it; then it wrote all the right answers on tests, and now this! I've got to see what this is all about.

As we approached the spot where the pen had been struck by lightning, the tiny piece of star could be seen. After brushing away the grass, its silvery color glinted in the afternoon sunshine. I could see Jasmine had a worried look as she cautioned,

"If what the pen wrote is really true, you and Edgar better stay far away from it."

The sparkling cubic centimeter entranced me. I stared at it almost hypnotically. Strangely enough, I could see a dim reflection of my mother's face in its glittering light.

"I must do it." I said, "We always hear about having courage and taking risks. Well, this is my chance to prove I have that courage. I have what it takes to face life. I just have to make this wish, and go inside the pen. It will be the greatest adventure into the unknown. Maybe, if I have enough faith, I will get a chance to see mother again."

"Jonathan, what are you babbling about?" Mother is dead; no one and no wish in the world can ever bring her back!" Jasmine said this in such a matter of fact and cold tone.

"I didn't say I would bring her back", I immediately responded, "But maybe the pen can take me to the unknown place, beyond death, where she now stays."

There was a moment of silence. I could see that Jasmine and Edgar felt a deep respect for my faith, and my willingness to go inside the pen. I clutched the piece of silver light in my hand, and looking beyond the blue; I said,

"Maybe I could see her just one last time; just to tell her how much I loved her, how much I miss her, and how my heart constantly aches to see her once again."

Edgar, with a surprise show of sentimentality, said,

"It's a noble and wonderful concept, Jonathan, but I think we've gone far enough. If you go inside that pen, you may never come back again." Determined, I said,

"It's a chance, a risk I've got to take." I could see Edgar was horrified at the idea that I would become liquid ink. Jasmine, with the wind in her long, black hair, pleaded with me,

"Please, Jonathan, don't do this."

It was too late. I hunkered down and picked up the star again. The white of my knuckles showed as I squeezed and made my wish. As I wished, I began to glitter like liquid silver; black hair and eyebrows turned white. Then, a swirl of blue wind whipped about me like a mini-tornado. A flash of light beamed forth, and then a puff of blue and silver smoke dissipated. With the smoke gone, it was evident I had disappeared. Frantically, Jasmine looked all about her. Suddenly, Edgar spied a small glass tube on the grass; it was corked and filled with blue ink! In utter horror, Edgar exclaimed,

"Look, it must be Jonathan!" Then Jasmine could not hold back her emotions, and said,

"Oh, Jonathan, what have you done? No one should die at thirteen years old! I love you, Jonathan, and I swear I'll find some way to get you back here."

Droplets of tears streamed down the cheeks of her face. She held the tube of ink in her slender fingers, and then she said to Edgar,

"Please, Edgar, think of something, please!"

As she spoke, I could hear her. I realized I was stuck inside this tube, and that I was liquefied into ink. But somehow I could still reason and think. I knew that I had to get out by the next sunrise or I would vaporize, and be gone forever!

Although Jasmine's emotions clouded her thinking, Edgar's keen mind remained calm and sharp as a razor. He thought of a brilliant solution. Then he said to Jasmine,

"Jasmine, don't worry, I have a brainstorm, and I know it will work." Then explained,

"It seems Jonathan has always been afraid to die, right? He's afraid of the unknown. He also misses his mother, terribly. I believe he wants to face his fear. He now has the courage and faith to enter an unknown realm, and in that unknown, it is your mother he wants to see."

"All of what you say is probably true", Jasmine agreed, "But that does not help us get him back."

"Just listen", he said calmly, "We will go to your father, explain this whole fantastic situation, and ask him to draw Jonathan into a painting that will allow him to escape the pen before the next sunrise."

With that said, Jasmine wrapped her grateful arms around Edgar, and gave him a big kiss on the cheek. Then she looked at him quite differently as she said,

"Edgar, you are a true genius, and more importantly, a true friend." His face blushed scarlet, and almost matched the color of his hair. For the first time, Jasmine looked beyond his pudgy face and freckles; she saw him for the depth of his heart, and the brilliance of his mind.

Chapter VII

Although this fantastic story amazed my father, he did not believe a shred of it. This would not be the first time Jasmine or Edgar pulled off a practical joke. Just to humor the kids, my Dad decided to do the drawing.

Edgar took out the pen, and Jasmine uncorked the ink filled tube. Carefully, Edgar stuck the golden point into the glass tube, and slowly pulled the side lever. As he did this, the pen sipped the ink, and I could feel myself being stretched and drawn into its dark, cavernous bladder. Indeed, it was terrifying.

My father began to draw with the magic golden pen. First he drew me. He sketched my body in no time. He gave me a blue denim jacket with matching blue jeans. Just as he completed putting red sneakers upon my feet, he noted a fantastic phenomenon! I began moving my arms and hands in a rapid up and down motion! Then I blinked my eyes, and my mouth began to open. All three gazed at me in awe and wonder. In a low echoing voice, Father, Jasmine, and Edgar could hear me speak. My voice spread throughout the molecules of the paper, and even the paper itself vibrated with each echo.

"Hello, hello . . . . ooo . . . . I'm, I'm, in, in another, other, other, . . . dimension . . . sion . . . sion." I said. My father sat in absolute amazement. He now understood this was not a practical joke. He realized I would need all his artistic skills to help me in my quest to face the unknown, and to perhaps see my mother one more time. Ultimately, it was me who would have to display the courage to escape this other dimension.

So all night, and into the wee hours of the morning, my Father, Jasmine, and Edgar thought of ways to help me face my fear of the unknown, and to overcome my fear of dying. Then, with only an hour before dawn, Edgar came up with a brilliant idea. And once again, Jasmine gave him a big kiss on the check. Edgar beamed like a bright star. And so, my father began to draw. He knew a person had to see beauty and truth, and had to experience love and kindness. These were the gifts and virtues that gave birth to courage and faith. Yes, these were the essences of the immortal soul. These were the blessings that gave one the power to hope, to face anything, and to accomplish anything!

Thus, he drew a glorious garden filled with the deepest violets and the bluest bluebells. Red roses bloomed and blew kisses in the golden sunlight, and laughing daffodils danced and nodded their heads in the wind. Red Cardinals and Bluebirds chirped and flitted from tree to tree. Robins hopped from field to field, and sparrows sang sweet melodious tunes. And when the forest was still, the unheard songs were even sweeter. A gentle blue-green sea surrounded this paradise. Mounds of foamy surf gently crashed upon a fresh, pink beach. Tall pine forests perfumed the air with the scent of sweetness and cedar, and purple mountains touched a hard, blue sky. The golden fields of wheat and barley undulated gently with the wind. Yes, the sun and rain kissed this paradise with the sweetest affection.

The people of this paradise only knew of love, truth, and kindness. They were unselfish, and did not know of jealousy. They did not know how to lie, and did not know about war. They had never heard of sickness or pain. And they would never die!

The garden was located on a cliff, but I was on another cliff. Between my cliff and the garden, an unfathomable abyss loomed as the eternal separation. The black expanse frightened me, but somehow I wanted to get to the other side . . . to the paradise!

In the heavens above, my father sketched a twinkling, silver-star. It was not unlike the one that fell onto the football field. I had to cross the blackness in order to reach the sunlit garden. I could never simply walk into the abyss; no . . . I had to have faith first. So, my father beamed a streak of silver light from the star to me. The light engulfed me like a blanket. It glowed brightly. It felt like all the world's love was pulsating through my body. With this faith in the beam of light, I gained courage. The ray of light extended from me, across the abyss, all the way to the wonderful paradise.

Chapter VIII

I actually began to walk upon a beam of light! As I walked, beads of sweat poured from my forehead and glistened on the cheeks of my face. Carefully, I inched my way upon this silver shadow. Suddenly, flakes of pure white snow gently descended. As each crystal touched me, I could feel the courage growing within me. Then, a steady wind began to blow harder and harder, and the snow and storm intensified. It was almost a blizzard now. I could barely see in front of me. Once my vision was impaired, I began to doubt my ability to make it to the other side. I started to slip from the beam of light. All at once, I lost my balance . . . . and fell! My body knifed through the darkness at incredible speed. My stomach turned upside-down, and I was about to let out a scream when, out of nowhere, someone gathered me into open arms. As I turned to look, white light illuminated from the face and body of the person holding me. It was an angel. It was my mother! As she held me in her heavenly arms, she said to me,

"Did you believe for one moment that I would let you fall? And after coming such a long way to visit me!"

"Mother, it's really you! Oh, Mother, you died so suddenly, and I felt I never got a chance to say goodbye to you. I mean a real proper goodbye. To tell you how much I have loved you, still love you, and what you mean to me." I exclaimed.

"Well, she said, "I am so happy to see my son, and I am so proud of the courage you've displayed, Jonathan."

"Do you really believe I am brave, Mother?' I asked.

"Jonathan", she said emphatically, "I know you are brave and courageous, and now you must realize it yourself. You do not know the strengths you posses. They are all there inside of you. Just allow them to surface." I thought about this, and then I asked her,

"Can't you come back for awhile, Mother?" With a sad face, she said,

"Jonathan, I've already passed that way; I have served my purpose, and can never go back. Every human being serves a special purpose on earth, and then returns back to his or her Creator."

"Maybe, I can stay here with you for awhile? Could I, Mother? Could I?" I asked.

"I'm afraid it's impossible." She said, "You see, you have an entire life to fulfill upon the earth. So many goals to achieve. So many people to love. And so much time to learn about wisdom and how to be loved." I looked at my mother with tears in my eyes, and I said,

"I understand, I truly understand, Mother."

"Good", she said, "You are becoming a wise young man already."

Then she swept me into her angelic arms, and flew me back to the beam of light. She said, "Have faith in yourself, Jonathan. Have faith in God! Now, walk across the abyss. We will meet again. To you, it will seem like a long time, but here in Paradise, it will be like the blink of an eye."

As I began walking on the beam of light, she drifted into puffy clouds with spears of white light descending from the heavens. I watched her until she disappeared. Then I heard her voice,

"Remember that I love you, Jonathan. And although you can't see me, I will be in your heart until we meet again. It will be sooner than you think."

"I love you, mother . . . . I love you!" I said.

I now felt a renewed strength within my heart and soul. But could I make it to the other side? Could I get back home? With each step, I gained more confidence. The new knowledge I possessed gave me an unbreakable spirit.

When I finally made that last step, and reached the cliff of the garden, the entire drawing emanated into a blinding, white light. I could feel myself being pulled from the entire scene! My father, Jasmine, and Edgar stepped back, and covered their eyes with trembling hands. As they peaked through opened fingers, the light faded, and out of a fog-like haze, I suddenly appeared! I was unharmed. I had overcome my fear of the unknown. As I embraced my father, Jasmine, and Edgar, the soft, red rays of dawn streamed through the windowpane. Splashes of pink washed the walls as well as our souls, and a renewed joy filled our hearts.

For now, I was exhausted and could hardly speak. Later on, I would tell them about the garden, the abyss, wisdom, and most of all about Mother!

Jasmine took the magic golden pen from my father, and declared,

"I believe it is time for us to let go of this pen." Edgar said, philosophically,

"Perhaps it was not the pen that was all magic. Perhaps you believed in it so deeply that it became magical."

That evening, Jasmine, Edgar, and I walked to the sea. It was winter in St. Ives, England. The air was cold and foggy, but the sea bathed us in a warm breeze. We walked to the beach, and I could almost hear my Mother's voice in the whispering wind. The water broke into curly, white waves. The sky was filled with enormous, clouds. As I faced the horizon, I could still see the Paradise in my mind. I could feel the face of God, and the spirit of my mother as streaks of light descended from the Heavens. I threw the pen, with all my might, and we watched it slowly sink into the green sea.

As we faced the horizon, someone grabbed me by the shoulder. It was Butch.

"Hand over that pen, stupid!" He shouted.

"It's too late. It's part of the sea, now." I said. Jasmine was about to say something, but I stopped her. I turned to her and I said, "I'll handle this, Jasmine.

"You'll handle what?" Butch demanded, "You can't handle anything, let alone me."

"I can handle life," I said, "you wouldn't understand." At that moment, Butch said,

"We'll see about that." Then, he tried to punch me in the nose. But like lightning I raised my hand and caught Butch's forearm. As I squeezed, he grimaced in pain. Then I said very softly, "I told you I can handle life . . . which means I can handle you. Don't make me have to prove it, Butch."

I let go, and Butch looked into the eyes of Jasmine, then Edgar, then back to me. He couldn't understand why but there was something very different about me. He turned around, and walked away. As he walked, I called out to him. I said,

"Butch, perhaps we can become friends one day; it is the only way to live, you know." He turned around briefly, and his face softened. And the sun sank down into the Atlantic Ocean.

Vocabulary for
The Magic Golden Pen.

Alternate—to perform by terms. Taking turns doing something.
Drenched—to wet thoroughly
Luminous—bright, clear
Phenomenon—the appearance of an unusual happening.
Coincidence—correspond exactly
Exquisite—refined and delicate
Unscathed—not injured, without harm
Hypothesis—something assumed based on evidence
Reprimand—to reprove or correct severely
Maneuver—skill in movement; especially military operations
Apprehensive—anxious or worry over the future
Glinted—sparkled or shined
Frantic—violently mad or distracted
Unfathomable—infinite depth, unending

Abyss—bottomless gulf
Sarcastic—biting, cutting remark

Comprehension Questions for The Magic Golden Pen

1. In the beginning of the story, Jonathan is in emotional pain. What is the cause of this emotional pain?
2. What did Jasmine and Jonathan buy at the antique store?
3. How are they going to share the pen?
4. What does Jasmine's and Jonathan's father do for a living?
5. Foreshadowing is when the author gives you a hint at the beginning of a story to let you know what might happen later on in the story. When Jasmine picks up the fountain pen, how is the magic of it foreshadowed?
6. The Protagonist of a story is the hero. It is the person you are hoping will reach his or her goal. Based on this definition, who is the Protagonist of this story?
7. Why did the principal of Blue Mountain School call Jasmine and Jonathan to the office?
8. Who discovers Jasmine's and Jonathan's secret about the pen? How did he do this?
9. When Jonathan makes his wish, What happens to him?
10. What special theme or lesson can one learn from this story?
11. What is the Setting of this story? (Time and Place)
12. An Antagonist is a person, or a thing, or something abstract that is trying to stop or hurt the Protagonist. Based on this definition, who or what is the Antagonist in The Magic Golden Pen? (Think about this one.)
13. Irony is when the unexpected happens in a story. Can you think of unexpected or surprise happenings in this story?
14. Do you think Jonathan has courage? Prove your answer using facts from the story.
15. In what ways does Edgar prove he is a good friend to both Jasmine and Jonathan?

16. In what ways does Jasmine show her love for her brother, Jonathan?

17. Symbolism is when an object stands for some idea or feeling. For example a wedding ring stands for eternal love because it is a circle and because a diamond lasts forever. Based on this definition, why is it that Jonathan's "Father" is the one who helps him? Who might Jonathan's father represent or symbolize.

18. If you have learned about Metaphor, Simile, and Personification at school, can you identify at least five uses of these types of figurative language from the story?

19. Why couldn't Jonathan's mother come back to earth with him?

20. Who might the old man at the beginning of the story symbolize?

21. Why does Jonathan feel bad for not standing up to Butch when Butch grabbed him in the school corridor?

22. At the end of the story, why is Jonathan now willing to stand up to Butch?

23. Why did Jasmine feel happy when the pen squirted Butch with the ink?

24. When the pen writes its poem to Butch how does it make you feel? Why?

25. Why did Jonathan throw the pen into the sea?

Poems

By Mark A. Dema, Ph.D

Fortitude

When life is dark with clouds and rain
Just stand and wait upon the shore;
With steadfast prayer you will sustain
The hurricane around your door.

And when the storm alas abates
And the gleaming sun breaks on through;
A flood of tears rush through the gates
To form a rainbow in the blue.

For life is not just joy or grief
It is in trusting everyday;
Your strength will come from your belief
God washes every tear away!

In the Golden Sunlight
In the golden sunlight
I first saw your lovely face.
On a cool, starry evening
I touched your soft satin and lace.

Oh, like the stars in the heavens
Our love twinkled and shined.
And like a perfect poem
Our hearts beat in rhythm and rhyme.

But no one ever told us
Love isn't forever
And if you don't steer it right,
It can die in the river . . .
The river of life,
Where dreams melt with the setting sun,
As darkness falls, and your soul is undone.

And although it is over,
And the sun is gone, today.
Perhaps, the rain will wash you clean
And the steel clouds will all drift away.

For no matter how far you try to run
You cannot pretend it was not real
For when your eyes and mine meet,
The angels will tell us what to feel.

In the golden sunlight
I first saw your lovely face.
But no one ever told us
Love isn't forever.

Living with an Alcoholic

We sat in fear most of the time,
At a time
When life should be sublime.
We never knew what to expect
Wind, rain, ice or fire!
When he was sober
Life was so good
Sweetly good,
Made me crawl out of my monkshood.
It was then we walked in confidence,
And the sun and moon made sense.

But when he drank
Until his speech was slurred
And the Devil gazed from his eyes,
Then we did not know what to expect.
Like a dark cloud overhead,
Ominous and threatening,
Violence now overshadowing.
The flowers and beams of light
That filtered through our eyes,
Eyes filled with sadness and salty tears.

I used to think in all those years
Everybody was better than me.
Because I was part of him
I didn't know
I was a separate entity.
And for what it's worth
That painful time
Indeed, gave birth
To deep dimensions
Of faith and trust,
For God helped me build castles
Out of rubble and dust!

The Old Man and Autumn

I met an old friend at the park,
Perhaps his age touched eighty-two;
So now the twilight patriarch,
Had lived his life and paid his due.

Age spots upon the pale, soft hands,
His voice piped wisdom's words so sweet;
Time-distant, emotional lands,
Where thoughts give feelings ice and heat.

An adored child who gave him life,
Then left his heart in bitter cold;
He then found love in one soft wife,
And like the dawn ascended bold.

Worldly things, we desire, we lust,
Like money, power, fleeting fame;
Earth's rock and flesh that turn to dust,
The wise old man tried to explain.

When we are young the days seem long,
Clouds move faster than father time;
The children sing a different song
For starry climes and souls sublime.

But, alas, the sun is setting fast,
Thus clarifies truth and meaning;
The corporeal world is vast,
But grace is the spirit's wellspring!

The Abuser

You tried to take
For your own sake
My strong self-esteem
What's at stake
Your own self-hate
Others you berate.

You hide behind
And try to find
Prestige with violence
Just a fake
Still on a binge
Who seeks revenge

You seek power
Every hour
Without substance
Evil deeds
No construction
Just destruction

When all is done
You'll have become
A shallow vessel
Without a soul
The grave your goal!

Life and Death

When I think
Of the centuries gone by
All those alone
Who lie in dust;
No physical trace,
Except the headstone's grace.
Date of birth, date of death,
Meaningless in time and space.

What is left behind,
To sustain the emptiness,
For lack of life force evidence,
And give some meaning
To those lives once in breath?
Perhaps the legacy of love . . . .
The little acts of kindness
That electrified the souls of others.

A faith that rippled
To distant shores;
The courage that found
The light of heaven
And made death's mighty blow
A bit softer
In the afterglow!

Long Before
Patrick Henry famed his words,
Hancock etched his name,
Lenny Bruce exposed the truth,
Martin conquered old Jim Crow.
Luther disbelieved a lie,
While Keats declared the truth.
Leonardo enraptured beauty,
Cleopatra captured the east,
Dylan demonstrated love,
And Jesus did it all!

Time and Dreams

Memories deep within my mind,
Family, friends, and youth sublime,
Their smiles fade like glowing sunsets,
Voices echo with no regrets.
What once was real is now a dream,
Past events, like rich, sweet cream.
Then savor every delight,
Till darkness overwhelms the light,
For what was once real . . .
Is now a dream.

The Sweetest Life

The sweetest life is filled with love,
Like children raining from above;
Each one like fluffy marigolds,
Blossoms golden and now unfolds.

Each child a miracle from God,
In our garden of earth and sod;
Now nurtured with sunshine and pain,
And growth from emotional rain.

We can't protect them forever,
But love lines never dissever;
If we give our breath completely,
And stand in shadows discreetly.

One day the child will hear the wind,
And the song of that sunshine friend;
Children like flowers from above,
Fragrance one's life with sweetest love!

True Love

When my eyes trace,
Upon your face,
Your sacred spirit,
Soft embrace
Like moonlight silk
And honey milk.

The hour is dark,
Before the lark,
Will sing once again,
Make its mark
I'll wait for you
On clouds in blue.

For love and time,
Do intertwine,
Shall not cease to be,
Forever
Within my heart
To never part!

The Dark Day

From the gray heavens,
Of a great distance
The rain falls
In glorified mists
Veils of persistence.
And the clouds weep,
And it is dark and bleak,
Inside the blackness of a dark sleep.
It weighs heavy
Upon my immortal soul.

From the Heavenly blue,
After the rain, I spy
Cool shafts of light
In celestial beams
A rainbow from the sky.
And my spirit seems light,
To break black clouds in respite,
The darkness now in flight.
It weighs heavy
Upon my immortal soul!

Remember When

The sixties sprinkled like the stars,
The high ideals of fenceless skies;
Jim Morrison would break on through,
The Hendrix watchtower did rise.

Upon the streets of Washington,
Dr. King climbed the mountaintop;
The march for civil rights was won,
And Viet Nam had just begun.

In civil right the law was writ,
Minorities would now be free;
But hope eroded bit by bit,
When housing came without a key.

A peace was made with hand-dove signs,
Make believe like plastic flowers;
But blood still flowed 'til eyes were blind,
And drugs decayed the flower power.

The Hippies screamed at big, fat cats,
Oh, they pressed for revolution;
But in mid-life became the rats,
The yuppies poised for prostitution.

For those of us who did not sell,
The high ideals in exchange for Hell;
Yes, those who sit in silent sound,
The poets who revere the ground.

Pass the truth to innocent child,
That worldly things disguise emotion;
Virtues will never cease in style,
And God's will be our devotion.

Tropical Impressions

Verdant needles of palm trees,
Sway, gracefully, against ice cream clouds
Into the soft, blue sky.
They dance upon the warm breeze,
While frothy waves recede to deep green;
And the wind whispers love songs
To the clear, bright sun.
Like twinkling stars that have come to rest,
After their diamond shine has been
Shattered and scattered
Upon the bosom of the ocean's breast,
Clear to the bottom of the sea
One can spy melted emeralds
Liquefied in crystal melody;
And the wind whispers love songs
To the clear, bright sun.
And the orange and yellow fish
Swim and laugh through a coral run . . .
And when the winter winds
Blow ever cold,
This sunny scenery will then unfold,
And dance upon that inner screen
Pure and sweet imagination!

When I Found Love

When I was young just one and twenty,
I pondered to know why I was born;
My feelings overwhelmed me plainly,
Oh, this world seemed so tattered and torn.

Yes, a world so poorly imperfect,
I searched myself, and the void inside;
Like a death knell when eulogistic,
In God's hands only could I abide.

As the dawn rose, my miracle came,
My infant daughter whose cries I heard;
Like the sun she set my soul aflame,
Never again could life seem absurd.

Those scorpion thoughts now in past tense,
For when I found love, all life made sense!

Birch Trees

The Birch trees in winter
Soft white, deep black
Bend to the ground
Enamored with crystal glass;
Now shine and sparkle profound
Surrounded by golden grass.

Green summer then descends
All blue, all gold
Birches kiss the earth
With long windy hair;
Like leafy ladies they befriend
The violets and roses fair.

Like slender models, kiss the sky
Leaves shimmer in sunshine
Dazzling to the human eye
Making man forget the clock;
To and fro in brilliance fine
Soft and white, deep and black!

Winter Poem

Light snow divine
White winged in lines
Blizzard winds blow cold.
Flakes so fine
Like the stars they gleam
Inside the moonlight beams.

When snowflakes cease
Blue skies increase
New north winds whistle.
Sunlight freezes
Ice clicks and sings
While church bells ring.

The Cause

My son died, today.
The Lieutenant said,
"Your son was killed in action;
He died defending a great cause."
Oh, I tried to catch my soul . . .
As it fell into the abyss,
Along with my knees,
As they battered the earth . . .
And the blood as it drained
From my hallowed face.
And my tears!
Oh, the infinite tears!
Dripping like large drops of rain.

What cause was he talking about?
"Are you sure it was my son;
It can't be my son", I said.
Was it greater than God's cause
When he planted my son
Into my womb?
And I felt the action of his
Tiny feet and hands!
Was it greater than the
Cause and effect
I felt at the moment of his birth?
That all embracing . . . all or nothing at all

Eternal love I felt for my son!

For certain as the stars and space above,
The cause could never be emptier
Than the emptiness . . . the hollow grave . . .
Inside the darkness of my heart.
For the cause will long be forgotten
Before my heart returns to dust . . .
Did I tell you?
My son died, today!

The Desire

The sun sets in the golden west,
And the night stars come to dream;
Steal away, then, nonetheless,
And we will climb a bright moonbeam.

I know we come from different lands,
Not someone you desire;
Please let me be your lead man,
And, then, I will light your fire.

Into a shower of bright stars
That gleam on the Milky Way;
Into the colors of Renoir,
If only you'd meet me halfway.

Then, like the dawn, all set in pink,
We'll melt into each other;
For life passes like a blink,
And sweet, sweet love we must gather!

The Children

A few years ago, they were not here,
Just quintessential stardust dear;
I look at all these new-born babes,
And then to stars in the astrolabe.

Tiny spirits once still in search,
For a clay home upon the earth;
Like small seeds scattered on the ground,
Sprouting to grassy blades profound.

They come in colors like the rainbow,
And brighten up this world of woe;
Like flowers they dress a cozy home,
And glitter like the stars in the astrodome.

A few years ago, they were not here,
Just quintessential stardust, Dear!

Together

In the pouring rain,
We cuddled
Under a black umbrella;
We kissed
With sacred lips
We could hear the rhythmic rain
And watched each silver drop
Hip, hop, pop
Off the silken street
You and I and skyscrapers, too
Soaring beyond the clouds
Into the blue.

A Sonnet: When Buildings Crumble

I saw a vacant building, hollow, now,
'Twas once filled with people, business, and work;
How unmowed lawns expound its empty bough,
To work there, one's name was framed in goldwork.

Yes, image and reputation for all,
Sunshine in one's dark room of one's dark life;
Power and prestige to erase the pall,
As if one building could remove the strife.

And now the stones crumble slowly into dust,
Still, my life retains its immortal soul;
For I rose above the bitter distrust,
And found no building could make me whole.

To work, to serve, to be just to others,
To be God's servant, and mankind's brother!

Miracles

Love is the force
That can create
A miracle.
Faith is the rose
That blossoms
From a seed of love!

Under snow and ice
Seemingly no device
And yet,
With the sun's sweet kisses
The spring's soft breeze
And God's gentle grace . . .
Blooms forth
Into glorious, red petals
Merely spun from earth,
Air, water, and sun.
One of many little miracles!

Childhood Neighborhood

I went back to my old neighborhood,
Where once I was a brash boy;
In my Astoria childhood,
I played stickball with Rob, Ron, and Roy.

As I looked to the gleaming window,
I could see my father's face;
He whistled for me loud and slow,
Alas, all's gone without a trace.

I gazed upon the school playground,
Where sunshine flooded my mind;
But the sun's moved west from eastbound,
And has left those times behind.

I recalled the Sycamore tree,
On a glorious summer day;
Where I sat with precious Mary,
While our hearts and lips found their way.

Although the buildings still remain,
The people I knew are gone;
In my mind I hear that song's refrain,
Love is the upper echelon.

Love is the ride I felt in space,
My vehicle back to childhood;
Makes each moment now fixed in space,
Makes my life more understood.

But just one more time . . . .
Oh, if I only could!

One Night

The rain came like cold ice cream sprinkles,
As we stayed in bed and pondered;
The sound of rain, deep pain, and wrinkles,
And our souls forever wandered.

Up to the stars so high in the sky,
And under the cozy, white sheets;
We pledged our love with a moonlit pie,
As you read Rossetti, and I Keats.

We vowed this kiss would always endure,
Always, my love, you'll have my heart;
Like rays of sun so sacred and pure,
Permeate the clouds in perfect art!

About the Author

This is Dr. Mark A. Dema's second book. His first book, Poetry Transcends Time, was well received throughout the Hudson Valley. His new book, The Magic Golden Pen and Poems, contains a beautiful story about a boy's quest for immortality as well as inspirational poetry.

Dr. Dema lives in the Hudson Valley with his wife Kristina, and his four year old daughter, Victoria. He is a N.Y. state certified teacher in Elementary Education grades K through 6, and English grades 7 through 12. He graduated from the State University at New Paltz, N.Y., and earned both his Bachelor of Science and his Master of Science degrees from that University. He earned his Doctorate from Cambridge State University in 2001. Mark is currently the Poet-in-Residence at Washingtonville Middle School and at Marlboro Middle School in New York. He teaches poetry through the beauty of the written word, and the magic of music. Mark utilizes his guitar and sings songs just as minstrels did hundreds of years ago throughout Asia and Africa, and Europe. He considers his work a vocation, and feels honored and humbled to touch the lives of so many students in such a special way.